Let's look at
Animals by Night

Created by
Claude Delafosse
and Gallimard Jeunesse
Illustrated by Héliadore

D0344126

*At the back of this book
you will find a press-out paper torch,
and a pocket to keep it in.*

FIRST DISCOVERY / TORCHLIGHT
MOONLIGHT PUBLISHING

At night, while you are tucked up asleep in your bed, there are lots of animals out and about in the dark.

In this book you can go out at night too, and see what they get up to!

Thanks to a simple torch made of paper, you can explore the dark pages of this book.
It's like magic!

You'll find the torch on the last page.
Press it out and slide it between the plastic page
and the black page underneath it. You'll be
amazed by what you light up!

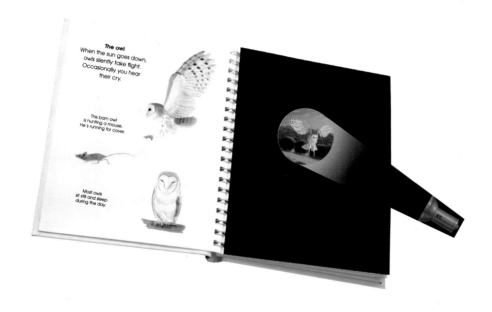

As you move it around,
little by little you'll discover
all the details hidden in each picture.

Many animals like to be awake and busy
during the day and asleep at night,
just as we do. There are others that
only wake up and go out after dark.
Let's find out who they are.

The owl

When the sun goes down,
owls silently take flight.
Occasionally you hear
their cry.

This barn owl
is hunting a mouse.
He's running for cover.

Most owls
sit still and sleep
during the day.

The cat

Cats like to go out
hunting by night. They walk
the rooftops in search
of a good meal –
a mouse or a small
bird perhaps.

Sometimes you
hear them miaowing
to other cats, telling
them they have
caught something
tasty.

Cats may be
sleepy during the day.
That's because
they've had
a busy night!

The moth

Have you noticed how some insects are drawn to lights after dark? Many of them are moths.

This giant peacock moth never flies by day. Its wings are patterned grey.

But this peacock butterfly is very colourful. It goes out during the day and rests at night.

The bat

Night has fallen.
The bat leaves its shelter
to look for food.

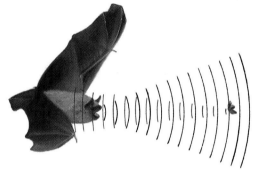

Bats are agile.
We don't know
what they see, but
they need their sonar
system to catch prey
and avoid objects
in the dark.

As morning comes,
they return home.
They hang upside down,
wrap their wings around
their body and sleep
through the day.

The mouse

Mice come out at night
and gather food.
These house mice find
all kinds of delicious things
lying around!

Later,
the mice return
to their holes.

This female
has three babies
to feed. She has to
eat a lot herself!

The hedgehog

These creatures
leave their burrows
as it gets dark.

Slug

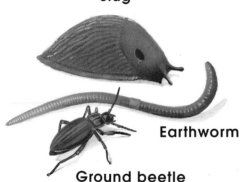

They root
in the ground
for small animals
like these. They also
eat larger animals –
snakes, frogs and mice.

Earthworm

Ground beetle

When hedgehogs
sense danger, they
curl up in a tight ball.
Then they are all spines!

Many other animals are nocturnal,
or active mainly at night.

Genet

Raccoon

Dormouse

Wild boar female, or sow

Young wild boar

Toad

Glis glis,
or fat dormouse

Dawn is breaking.
The animals that
have been so busy
through the night
will now sleep.

Other animals
are waking up.
It's the beginning
of a new day.

These details are from the dark pages of the book.

Can you find them using your magic torch?

FIRST DISCOVERY: OVER 125 TITLES AVAILABLE IN 5 SERIES

AMERICAN INDIANS
ANIMAL CAMOUFLAGE
ANIMALS IN DANGER
BABIES
BEARS
THE BEAVER
THE BEE
BEING BORN
BIRDS
BOATS
THE BODY
THE BUILDING SITE
THE BUTTERFLY
THE CASTLE
CATHEDRALS
CATS
CHRISTMAS AND NEW YEAR
CLOTHES AND COSTUMES
COLOURS
COUNTING
THE CROCODILE
THE DESERT
DINOSAURS
DOGS
DUCKS
THE EAGLE
EARTH AND SKY
THE EARTH'S SURFACE
THE EGG
THE ELEPHANT
FARM ANIMALS
FINDING A MATE
FIREFIGHTING
FLOWERS
FLYING
FOOTBALL
THE FROG
FRUIT
GROWING UP
HALLOWEEN
THE HEDGEHOG
HOMES

THE HORSE
HOW THE BODY WORKS
THE INTERNET
THE JUNGLE
THE LADYBIRD
LIGHT
THE LION
MONKEYS AND APES
MOUNTAINS
THE MOUSE
MUSIC
ON WHEELS
THE OWL
PENGUINS
PICTURES
PIRATES
PREHISTORIC PEOPLE
PYRAMIDS
RABBITS
THE RIVERBANK
THE SEASHORE
SHAPES
SHOPS
SMALL ANIMALS IN THE HOME
SPORT
THE STORY OF BREAD
THE TELEPHONE
THE TIGER
TIME
TOWN
TRAINS
THE TREE
UNDER THE GROUND
UP AND DOWN
VEGETABLES
VOLCANOES
WATER
THE WEATHER
WHALES
THE WIND
THE WOLF

FIRST DISCOVERY / ATLAS
ANIMAL ATLAS
ATLAS OF ANIMALS IN DANGER
ATLAS OF CIVILIZATIONS
ATLAS OF COUNTRIES
ATLAS OF THE EARTH
ATLAS OF FRANCE
ATLAS OF ISLANDS
ATLAS OF PEOPLES
ATLAS OF SPACE
PLANT ATLAS

FIRST DISCOVERY / ART
ANIMALS
HENRI MATISSE
THE IMPRESSIONISTS
LANDSCAPES
THE LOUVRE
PABLO PICASSO
PAINTINGS
PAUL GAUGUIN
PORTRAITS
SCULPTURE
VINCENT VAN GOGH

FIRST DISCOVERY / TORCHLIGHT
LET'S LOOK AT ANIMALS BY NIGHT
LET'S LOOK AT ANIMALS UNDERGROUND
LET'S LOOK AT ARCHIMBOLDO'S PORTRAITS
LET'S LOOK AT CASTLES
LET'S LOOK AT CAVES
LET'S LOOK AT DINOSAURS
LET'S LOOK AT FAIRIES, WITCHES, GIANTS AND DRAGONS
LET'S LOOK AT FISH UNDERWATER
LET'S LOOK AT LIFE BELOW THE CITY
LET'S LOOK AT INSECTS
LET'S LOOK AT THE JUNGLE
LET'S LOOK AT THE SKY
LET'S LOOK AT THE ZOO BY NIGHT
LET'S LOOK FOR LOST TREASURE
LET'S LOOK INSIDE THE BODY
LET'S LOOK INSIDE PYRAMIDS
LET'S LOOK FOR LOST TREASURE

FIRST DISCOVERY CLOSE-UPS
LET'S LOOK AT THE GARDEN CLOSE UP
LET'S LOOK AT THE HEDGE CLOSE UP
LET'S LOOK AT THE OAK CLOSE UP
LET'S LOOK AT THE POND CLOSE UP
LET'S LOOK AT THE RAINFOREST CLOSE UP
LET'S LOOK AT THE SEASHORE CLOSE UP
LET'S LOOK AT THE STREAM CLOSE UP
LET'S LOOK AT THE VEGETABLE GARDEN CLOSE UP
LET'S LOOK UNDER THE STONE CLOSE UP

Translator: Clare Best   - Editorial adviser: Sarah Heath
ISBN 1 85103 282 7
© 1997 by Editions Gallimard Jeunesse
English text © 1998 by Moonlight Publishing Ltd
First published in the United Kingdom 1998
by Moonlight Publishing Limited, The King's Manor, East Hendred, Oxon. OX12 8JY
Printed in Italy by Editoriale Lloyd